GUIDE TO THE LONG PATH

2nd Edition, 1987

Published By

New York-New Jersey Trail Conference
232 Madison Avenue
New York, NY 10016
Copyright 1987
ISBN: 0-9603966-4-0

THE LONG PATH

The first suggestion for a "Long Brown Path" from New York City to the Adirondacks was not for a continuous, marked trail with a specific beginning and end. The idea for this trail originated in the early 1930's with Vincent J. Schaefer of the Mohawk Valley Hiking Club and his brother Paul, who proposed that New York State establish its own "Long Path" similar to the Long Trail in Vermont. The original idea was for an unmarked route through a ten-mile corridor in the back country to be followed on topographical maps.

The name of the path came from the weekly column in the New York Post by Raymond Torrey, one of the authors of the original New York Walk Book. In a series of articles, Mr. Torrey described the original trail route as having been scouted by W. W. Cady from the George Washington Bridge to Gilboa and by Vincent Schaefer from Gilboa to the northern Adirondacks.

In 1935, property for the Palisades Interstate Parkway started to be acquired, and its construction (increasing accessibility of the Palisades cliffs) renewed interest in the Long Path project. The original proposal was to use the Northville-Lake Placid Trail, built a few years earlier by the Adirondack Mountain Club (ADK), as the northernmost part of the Long Path. W. W. Cady of New York assisted in the project south of the Catskills, and some marking was done. However, after several years, the momentum was lost, and the project lay dormant for many years. In 1960 Robert Jessen of the Ramapo Ramblers urged revival of the project and began field work from New York City to the Catskills.

The 2" x 4" aqua/blue blazes of the Long Path generally follow mountain ridges, but occasionally cross valleys and lowlands. The route is along wooded trailway for as much as possible, but it goes along paved roads out of necessity in several sections. It starts at the New Jersey side of the George Washington Bridge and continues along the top of the Palisades. After traversing Hook Mountain and High Tor, it swings west into Harriman State Park and onto the Ramapo Rampart. It cuts across the escarpment of Schunemunk Mountain and then the farmland beyond. The bluff of the Shawangunks in Minnewaska State Park is the next height of land. Descending to cross Roundout Valley, the trail enters the Catskill Forest Preserve. There it crosses Peekamoose, Slide, Blackhead, Windham High Peak, and other great mountains of the area. The northern terminus of the Long Path is now at Windham. Beyond the Catskills, across the Mohawk Valley, and up to the Adirondacks, the route is in the planning stages, with construction north of Windham possibly starting this year.

ACKNOWLEDGMENTS

This guide to the Long Path has been made possible by support from the Archbold Charitable Trust. The Archbold family's commitment to outdoor preservation for public enjoyment has enabled the New York-New Jersey Trail Conference, a nonprofit volunteer organization, to accelerate the Long Path project and provide this handbook.

For over 20 years the Trail Conference has been working to create the Long Path in the State of New York. Because of its length, complex problems arise when such a trail must pass through private and public lands. The Archbold Trust has enabled the Trail Conference to survey alternate routes, as well as research and obtain permission from landowners and state officials. This work has been spearheaded by a trail consultant, while volunteers construct the trail by flagging, building, and blazing the Long Path. Volunteer clubs of the Trail Conference are responsible for the ongoing maintenance of the Trail.

As time goes by, the work of trail preservation in heavily populated states like New York becomes more urgent. Given the opportunity to carry on a project of this scope at this critical time, the New York-New Jersey Trail Conference thanks the Archbold Charitable Trust for their generous gift to the public.

Additional thanks to:

James A. Ross--Long Path Project Supervisor
Albert Field--Long Path Consultant, Field Route, and Trail Description
George Zoebelein--Field Checking, Maps
Richard S. Ringel--Maps
Earl Albright--Maps
Nat Lester--Map Updates for Trail Route
H. Neil Zimmerman--Catskill Coordination
JoAnn Dolan--Inspiration
Cheryl Parks--Word Processing Service
Howard J. Dash--Editing
Bruce Scofield--Production
Robert Cresko--Cover Design
Trail Volunteers of the NY-NJ Trail Conference

HIKING THE LONG PATH

Hiking the Long Path takes the hiker from an urban metropolis to the remote wilderness 200 miles northward. As of this writing, it is possible to hike all of the trail but not to camp out in all sections: Park regulations, restrictions through private lands, and miles along roads preclude it.

The Long Path Guide is written with a south-to-north description. Every attempt has been made to make it explicit enough so that a hiker going from north to south can also follow the route without much difficulty.

The sections are divided so that each can be hiked in a day's time. Information is given in each section of this guide on the facilities and services available along the way. To supply water there are springs and streams along the trail; however, the water is untested and precaution must be taken to purify it for drinking.

The access directions to the trailheads are at the beginning of each section. They are only suggestions; it is likely that there are other ways to arrive at the trailhead.

Eight maps are included with this guide, listed as LP in the index. The index of supplementary maps also includes those available commercially. These include hiker map sets published by the New York-New Jersey Trail Conference listed under each section as TC. These map sets include Harriman-Bear Mountain Trails (TC Maps 3 & 4), West Hudson Trails (TC Map 8), Shawangunk Trails (TC Map 9), and Catskill Trails (TC Maps 40-43).

Maps in the New York Walk Book (5th edition, available from the Trail Conference) are listed as WB. Hiker's Region Maps published by Walking News, Inc. (P.O. Box 352, New York, NY 10013) are listed as HR.

The Long Path is marked with aqua blazes. However, in the Catskills, the route follows trails maintained by the New York State Department of Environmental Conservation and the color of markers vary. RED-marked trails usually run from east to west; BLUE-marked trails, from south to north; and YELLOW-marked trails are side trails, link trails, or run diagonally. See the introduction to Section 14 for directions in following the Long Path in the Catskills. There is, at this time, a gap in the continuity of the trail. Section 20, from Platte Clove Road to Palenville in the Catskills, is missing. However, construction is underway and should be completed in the spring of 1987.

At selected trail junctions the Long Path is marked with round, blue plastic markers bearing the Long Path logo, a sample of which appears on the inside cover page.

Much of the trail is on private land; do not give any landowner reason to regret having given us permission to cross it. Build no fires except at established, official camp sites.

Litter should not be buried! (Animals will dig it up.) Everything you carry in should be carried out. Human waste should be buried at least 150 feet from water, trail, or campsite.

Sections - Mileage

	From	To	Miles	Cumulative
1	George Washington Bridge	N.Y. State Line	11.9	11.9
2	N.Y. State Line	Nyack--Route 59	9.1	21.0
3	Nyack--Route 59	Long Clove--Route 9-W	7.7	28.7
4	Long Clove--Route 9-W	Mount Ivy--Route 202	6.4	35.1
5	Mount Ivy--Route 202	Seven Lakes Drive	9.4	44.5
6	Seven Lakes Drive	Long Mountain Parkway	10.1	54.6
7	Long Mountain Parkway	Woodbury--Route 32	11.3	65.9
8	Woodbury--Route 32	Salisbury Mills--Route 94	9.8	75.7
9	Salisbury Mills--Route 94	Rock Tavern--Route 207	7.3	83.0
10	Rock Tavern--Route 207	Montgomery--Route 17K	7.2	90.2
11	Montgomery--Route 17K	Ulsterville--Route 52	11.0	101.2
12	Ulsterville--Route 52	Route 44-45/Jenny Lane	16.5	117.7
13	Route 44-55/Jenny Lane	Catskill Park-Riggsville	13.5	131.2
14	Catskill Park-Riggsville	Bull Run	8.7	139.9
15	Bull Run	Denning Road	7.5	147.4
16	Denning Road	Woodland Valley	11.1	158.5
17	Woodland Valley	Phoenicia	6.3	164.8
18	Phoenicia	Lake Hill--Route 212	11.6	176.4
19	Lake Hill--Route 212	Platte Clove Road	13.3	189.7
20	Platte Clove Road	Palenville	-	-
21	Palenville	North Lake	5.5	195.2
22	North Lake	Batavia Kill	11.2	206.4
23	Batavia Kill	Windham--Route 23	9.5	215.9

SECTION 1   George Washington Bridge to N.Y.-N.J. State Line

FEATURE:	Palisades	**MAPS:**	LP Map #1A
			TC Map --
DISTANCE:	11.9 miles		WB Map #4
			HR Map #24

GENERAL DESCRIPTION:

The Long Path runs between the Palisades Interstate Parkway and the top of the Palisades, all on state land.   It is basically level, with a few short rises, until it crosses the N.Y. state line, where it descends steeply and then returns to the upper level.

Much of the land was formerly occupied by private estates, and the story of how it was acquired for public use is told in the **New York Walk Book**.   Today the only signs of the earlier use are the remains of walls, foundations, and driveways.

The Shore Path parallels the Long Path from south of the George Washington Bridge (GWB) all the way to the New York state line, and circular hikes can be taken via one of the paths that connect the top with the shore:

    0.3 Carpenters Stairs
    1.8 Palisades Avenue
    5.1 Huyler Trail
    7.3 Alpine Approach Road
    9.9 Women's Federation Trail

It is also possible to make a circular trip by going out to Route 9-W and taking a bus back:

    0.5 Footbridge to southern end of Parkway
    1.2 Allison Rd. (on Hudson Terrace jog left a short block to reach 9-W)
    4.6 Greenbrook Rd.
    7.1 Tunnel to Closter Dock Rd.
    9.8 Footbridge to Camp Alpine

FACILITIES:

Parking -   Fort Lee Historic Park (closes at dusk), approx. 1 block south of
                the trailhead at the GWB, off Hudson Terrace (0.0 mi.)
           -   Metered parking at the trailhead on Hudson Terrace (0.0 mi.)
           -   Allison Park, when open (1.2 mi.)
           -   Rockefeller Lookout, limited to 20 min. (2.8 mi.)
           -   Alpine Lookout, limited to 20 min. (5.7 mi.)
           -   New Jersey headquarters, Palisades Interstate Park (7.6 mi.)
           -   State Line Lookout (10.2 mi.)
           -   Lamont-Doherty Geological Observatory Road (11.9 mi.)

Water   -   Gas station (1.0 mi.)
           -   Allison Park (1.2 mi.)
           -   Park office (7.6 mi.)
           -   State Line Lookout (10.2 mi.)

FACILITIES: (Cont'd)

Food	– Vending machines at gas station (1.0 mi.)
	– Snack bar at State Line Lookout (10.2 mi.)
Phone	– Gas station (1.0 mi.)
	– Palisades Ave. (1.8 mi.)
	– Closter Dock Road (7.1 mi.)
	– Park headquarters (7.6 mi.)
	– State Line Lookout (10.2 mi.)
Lodging	– Ft. Lee (0.0 mi.)

ACCESS:

From New York City, cross the GWB to the New Jersey side, and from the north, south, and west use any access road to the GWB: I-95, Routes 4, 46, 9-W, or the Palisades Interstate Parkway. The trail begins at the north pedestrian walkway of the George Washington Bridge at Hudson Terrace. Bus service (Red & Tan Route 9) runs along Route 9-W.

* * * * *

TRAIL DESCRIPTION

0.0 The Long Path begins on the N.J. side of the George Washington Bridge and is designated by three blue blazes on a large rock at the stairway to the north walkway over the Palisades Interstate Parkway. Climb the steps and enter the park. Follow the wide main path toward the Hudson River and then, near the top of the cliff, turn left and parallel the river.

0.3 Carpenters Stairs on the right lead steeply down to the shoreline.

0.5 On the left, a footbridge spans the northbound Parkway and leads to city streets. Soon afterward, note the old cannon mounted on your right.

1.0 Pass a gas station on the Parkway at your left.

1.2 After going left along the fence, the trail uses the roadway to Allison Park, which was developed by the trustees of the Estate of William Outis Allison (1849-1924) who was born and spent his life nearby. When it is open, the park offers water and rest rooms as well as picnic benches and overlooks. The trail follows Allison Park Road to a narrow strip of greenery between the Parkway and the road to St. Peter's College. It is briefly on the shoulder of the Parkway before re-entering the woods.

1.8 Descend a few yards to Palisade Avenue, then cross it and go up stairs to right. (Route 9-W is visible to the left; to the right the road goes to the shoreline. There is a sidewalk and a separate trail down.)

2.8 Rockefeller Lookout is opposite the northern tip of Manhattan at Spuyten Duyvil.

3.6 Clinton Point is one of the many fine outlooks across the river.

4.6 Cross over entrance road to Greenbrook Sanctuary (a private park for members only; see the **Walk Book**). The trail parallels the fence.

5.1   On the right is the upper end of Huyler Trail (red). This goes steeply down to Henry Hudson Drive and continues to its terminus on the Shore Path. The British may have climbed the cliff here in 1776.

5.8   Alpine Lookout is opposite the City of Yonkers.

7.1   The tunnel to the left leads to Rt. 9-W at Closter Dock Rd. (no parking here).

7.3   Go under Alpine Dock Road and turn left. The trail right goes down to the Alpine Boat Basin and picnic grounds.

7.6   The former Oltman House is now the New Jersey headquarters of the Palisades Park.

9.3   Cross former Ruckman Road near the (fenced) overlook at the cliff.

9.7   The trail left leads to a footbridge over the Parkway to the entrance of Camp Alpine of the Boy Scouts of America (emergency phone here).

9.9   Women's Federation Castle, dedicated in 1929 to the New Jersey State Federation of Women's Clubs for their work in establishing the Palisades Interstate Park. Take care for the blue and white Boy Scout trail which joins the Long Path, shortly turns right and descends to the Hudson River.

10.2 Continue to the right on concrete entrance road to State Line Lookout. (This was formerly Route 9-W.) At 532 feet, this is the highest point of the New Jersey Palisades. Beyond the rest rooms and snack bar, the trail follows the road briefly before turning right on a wide path that is a ski trail in winter.

11.2 State Line Monument. The trail goes through the fence to High Gutter Point (from which wood used to be sent down to be burned by steamships). The trail descends steeply, partly on steps rebuilt in 1981, and is joined by the northern end of the Shore Path (white). Turn left, uphill, and continue, turning right to Route 9-W.

11.9 Reach Rt. 9-W near Lamont-Doherty entrance road. (The Geological Observatory is part of Columbia University and entrance is not allowed.)

SECTION 2 New York State Line to Nyack—Route 59

FEATURE: Tallman Mountain	**MAPS:** LP Map #1B, 2

FEATURE: Tallman Mountain

DISTANCE: 9.1 miles

MAPS: LP Map #1B, 2
TC Map —
WB Map —
HR Map #24, (2/8)

GENERAL DESCRIPTION:

In this section the Long Path is partly in the woods and partly on roads. It goes through Tallman Mountain State Park and Blauvelt State Park as well as the Village of Piermont.   The trail continues north along the Palisades, paralleling Route 9-W.

FACILITIES:

Parking – Lamont-Doherty Geological Observatory Road, limited (0.0 mi.)
          – Tallman Mountain State Park, fee to enter during the season
             (2.0 mi.)
          – Piermont (3.0 mi.)
          – Town of Orangetown Park (5.9 mi.)
          – Nyack (9.1 mi.)

Water   – Tallman Mountain State Park, in season (2.0 mi.)
          – Piermont (3.0 mi.)
          – Nyack (9.1 mi.)

Food   – Tallman Mountain State Park, in season (2.0 mi.)
          – Piermont (3.0 mi.)
          – Nyack (9.1 mi.)

Phone   – Tallman Mountain State Park, in season (2.0 mi.)
          – Piermont (3.0 mi.)
          – Nyack (9.1 mi.)

Lodging – None

ACCESS:

The trailhead at Lamont-Doherty is on Route 9-W, just north of the NY-NJ state line. Take the Palisades Parkway to the Route 9-W exit (Exit 4); go north.

* * * * *

TRAIL DESCRIPTION:

0.0   From the Lamont-Doherty entrance road, go north (downhill), then enter woods and descend, rejoining the highway at the bottom of the hill.

0.8   Traffic light; road left is Oak Tree Rd., right is Washington Spring Rd., village of Palisades.

1.0   Go right on gravel road on state land. Watch for left turn across part of an old oil tank farm, walking along the edge of the berms and then back onto road.

2.0   Enter picnic area of Tallman Mountain State Park. (The swimming pool is open in season.) Zigzag through the park and finally descend steeply into Piermont.

3.0   Cross Sparkill Creek on the right-hand bridge, Ferdon Ave., and continue on Piermont Ave. past the war memorial. Turn left onto Tate Rd., which curves to the right. Go up steps to left. (The abandoned railroad grade is a local trail.) On Ash St., turn left; follow it uphill. Take the left fork to cross 9-W, go a few yards further left, then turn uphill on Highland Ave. (Tweed Boulevard). The road immediately turns right and parallels the highway (Route 9-W).

4.1   Watch for a sharp left turn uphill to plateau with Rockland Cemetery. Follow paved road around to right. (John C. Fremont, explorer, soldier, and candidate for U.S. President--"The Pathfinder"--is buried here as well as J.H Gorringer, whose exploit of bringing Cleopatra's Needle to America is pictured on his monument.) Watch for trail on right leading into the woods and down from the ridge.

5.9   Cross Clausland Mountain Rd. and the parking lot of Orangetown Park. The trail uses a dirt road, turns right and passes a water impoundment, once part of a military (World War I) rifle range. Across the stream, it is again on a dirt road.

6.9   Enter Blauvelt State Park. The long concrete galleries were part of an extensive small arms range during World War I and may serve as emergency shelters.

7.6   Turn left on Tweed Boulevard over knoll.

7.8   As the highway turns left, continue ahead on unused road. After passing a water tank on right and talus on left, footway becomes So. Highland Avenue.

8.4   Pass large houses and Nyack Missionary College on right. Go through gateway and turn left up Bradley Rd. In 50 yards, turn sharp right at driveway and ascend shoulder to ridge.

8.8   Turn right on unbuilt city street along fence behind houses to stub of Towt Rd. Descend. (There is no parking here.)

8.9   Waldron Ave. enters on left and turns north. Follow it.

9.1   Intersection of Waldron Ave. and Route 59. The trail continues over Thruway bridge ahead. Nyack is downhill to the right.

SECTION 3   Nyack--Route 59 to Long Clove--Route 9-W

FEATURE: Hook Mountain	**MAPS:** LP Map #2

DISTANCE: 7.7 miles

MAPS: LP Map #2
TC Map --
WB Map --
HR Map #(2/8)

GENERAL DESCRIPTION:

This section begins in Nyack where the trail goes along streets, with the exception of a short wooded stretch, until it turns off and ascends Hook Mountain. It then follows along the ridge overlooking the Hudson River and descends to Long Clove.

FACILITIES:

Parking   -   Nyack (0.0 mi.), (1.6 mi.)
             -   Christian Herald Road at Route 9W (1.6 mi.)
             -   Rockland Lake State Park--Long Clove (4.7 mi.)

Water   -   Nyack (0.0 mi.)
          -   Rockland Lake State Park, in season (4.7 mi.)

Food   -   Nyack (0.0 mi.)
         -   Rockland Lake State Park, in season (4.7 mi.)

Phone   -   Nyack (0.0 mi.)
          -   Christian Herald Road at Route 9W (1.6 mi.)
          -   Rockland Lake State Park, in season (4.7 mi.)

Lodging   -   Nyack (0.0 mi.)

ACCESS:

New York State Thruway, exit 11, west on Route 59 to the intersection with Mountainview Avenue (McDonald's is beyond the intersection on the left). The Long Path turns northward.

* * * * *

TRAIL DESCRIPTION:

0.0   Cross Thruway on Mountainview Avenue. In several hundred yards, the trail goes right, then left and right again, and up a gravel road to the backyards of townhouses, which are followed along the top of ridge. Watch for turnoff downhill.
1.3   Turn right (downhill) on Christian Herald Road.
1.6   Turn left on Route 9-W.
1.9   Watch for right jog marked on telephone pole. Trail begins easily but then climbs steeply up Hook Mountain on state land.
2.7   Rocky summit of Hook Mountain (729 ft.) with view in all directions. The trail continues along the ridge.

4.7 After an extremely steep descent, cross Rockland Landing Road. (To the
     left is Rockland State Park; to the right the road leads down to the
     Nyack Shore Trail.) The trail ascends from the gap past a family
     cemetery.
5.0 Trough Hollow. Trail returns to ridge.
7.7 After a steep descent, the section ends in Long Clove on Route 9-W just
     east of the junction with Route 304.

SECTION 4 Long Clove--Route 9-W to Mount Ivy--Route 202

		MAPS:	LP Map #2
FEATURE:	High Tor		TC Map --
DISTANCE:	6.4 miles		WB Map --
			HR Map #(2/8)

GENERAL DESCRIPTION:

Beginning at Route 9-W, the trail in this section follows roads until it ascends High Tor and follows the ridge to South Mountain. The section ends at Mount Ivy, ending the Long Path's traverse of the Palisades.

FACILITIES:

Parking – Long Clove Road (0.1 mi.)
– South Mountain Road, limited (1.0 mi.)
– Central Highway, limited (4.3 mi.)
– Mount Ivy, in the commuter lot on nonbusiness days. Phone the Haverstraw Police (914) 354-1500 and give them the car license number; have a Trail Conference decal in the window (6.4 mi.).

Water – Mount Ivy (6.4 mi.)

Food – Mount Ivy (6.4 mi.)

Phone – Mount Ivy (6.4 mi.)

Lodging – None

ACCESS:

Route 9-W to Long Clove Road, south of Haverstraw.

* * * * *

TRAIL DESCRIPTION:

0.0 From Rt. 9-W, go north on Long Clove Road, which immediately turns west; it becomes Scratchup Road when it again turns north to pass the quarry.

1.0 Turn right on South Mountain Road. Just past the access road from quarry below on the right, go left steeply up into the woods.

1.6 Pass white blaze of Deer Trail on right. (This trail descends .3 miles in the woods to reach Route 9-W opposite Wholesale Auto, about .8 miles by road to crossing of South Mountain Road.) Climb steeply five levels higher.

1.9 High Tor, 832 ft., is the highest point on the Palisades. Used by colonists as a signal point during the Revolution, it was later the site of an airplane beacon (of which only traces remain). This peak was the subject of Maxwell Anderson's play High Tor and was saved from destruction for trap rock by conservationists. The ridge became state property in 1943. The ends of the diabase columns form a polygonal pattern in the rock.

To the north the river vanishes behind Dunderberg. Across from Tomkins
Cove is Con Edison's Indian Point nuclear plant. To the south, the
Hudson River curves behind Hook Mountain. To the right is De Forest
Lake, crossed by Congers Road. To the west, the tower is on Jackie Jones
Mountain on the Ramapo Rampart in Harriman Park.
The trail descends steeply but then becomes a fire road all the way to
Central Highway.

3.2   The white-blazed trail leads to the right to the top of Little Tor.

4.3   Cross Central Highway in South Mountain Park (Rockland County). The
      trail becomes a footpath leading over a grassy summit to the top of an
      old quarry that overlooks Mount Ivy. Descend.

6.4   Turn right (downhill) on Route 45 into Mount Ivy, where Route 202 goes
      under Palisades Interstate Parkway.

SECTION 5   Mount Ivy--Route 202 to Seven Lakes Drive (Lake Skannatati)

FEATURE: Harriman State Park, southern half   **MAPS:**   LP Map #2, 3
                                                                   TC Map #3
DISTANCE: 9.4 miles   WB Map #5
                                                                   HR Map #17
GENERAL DESCRIPTION:

This section and the next one are detailed on the Harriman-Bear Mountain Park
maps published by the NY-NJ Trail Conference. The trail parallels the Parkway
for over a mile before climbing to Cheesecote Pond and down to Calls Hollow
Road. It then uses the Old Turnpike Trail, the buried cable route, and the
former Skannatati Trail to Seven Lakes Drive.

FACILITIES:

> **Parking**   -   Mount Ivy, in the commuter lot on nonbusiness days. Phone the
> Haverstraw Police (914) 354-1500 and give them the license
> number; have a NY-NJ Trail Conference decal in the window (0.0
> mi.).
>   -   Lake Skannatati (9.5 mi.)
>
> **Water**   -   Mount Ivy (0.0 mi.)
>   -   Streams (4.4 mi.)
>
> **Food**   -   Mount Ivy (0.0 mi.)
>
> **Phone**   -   Mount Ivy (0.0 mi.)
>
> **Camping**   -   Big Hill Shelter (5.3 mi.)

ACCESS:

Palisades Interstate Parkway
> Going north: Exit 11, take Route 45 north to junction with Route
> 202.
> Going south: Exit 12, Mt. Ivy.

* * * * *

TRAIL DESCRIPTION:

0.0   Start at the junction of Routes 202 and 45. Go under the Palisades
     Interstate Parkway and follow the entrance ramp to the right beyond
     Quaker Road to the triangle. Cross to the north side.
0.3   Enter the woods and parallel the Parkway.
1.3   Turn right on grassy road; at junction, bear sharply to the left and
     cross the south branch of the Minisceongo Creek.
1.4   Turn right onto woods road. Watch for trail turning left up hill to the
     knob.

1.7 Reach the knob with view of the Hudson. Descend far side and immediately turn right on woods road. When it intersects a better road, turn left uphill. This is the old Letchworth Road.

2.5 Pass along south and west sides of Cheesecote Pond. (Parking here is for residents of Haverstraw only.) Take the gravel road west, and then north away from the pond, then down and west again. Pass under power lines and along the edge of the Letchworth Village Cemetery.

3.2 Turn left on Calls Hollow Road (parking here is at your own risk). Just as the road makes a bend to the left, enter the woods to the right and cross creek. Go uphill, left, on a very old woods road (Turnpike Trail).

4.4 After crossing several small crests, reach a gravel road above buried cable and follow it ahead and gradually up. Water can be found along this section.

5.1 Cross the Suffern-Bear Mountain (SBM) Trail (yellow blazes) at the crest.

5.3 The Big Hill Shelter is 0.13 mi. to the left. Continue, following former Skannatati Trail.

5.9 At the paved road, go right and immediately turn right again into the woods.

7.7 Cross Lake Welch Drive at the junction with St. John's Road.

8.2 Pass the trailhead of the Beech Trail, blue blazes. The Beech Trail angles off to the right on its way to the Red Cross Trail. The Long Path veers left as it continues winding through the woods.

9.0 Cross Route 106 (former Route 210).

9.4 Pass Lake Askoti and cross Seven Lakes Drive to Lake Skannatati and parking area.

SECTION 6   Seven Lakes Drive to Long Mountain Parkway

FEATURE: Harriman State Park, northern half

DISTANCE: 10.1 miles

GENERAL DESCRIPTION:

MAPS: LP Map #3
TC Map #4
WB Map #5, 6
HR Map #17, 16

The route of the Long Path continues through Harriman State Park and crosses the Appalachian Trail in this section. The terrain varies as the trail climbs mountains, crosses trails, and passes swampy areas.

FACILITIES:

Parking – Lake Skannatati (0.0 mi.)
– Lake Tiorati Circle, right uphill from where the trail crosses Arden Valley Road (6.8 mi.)
– Long Mountain Parkway (10.0 mi.)

Water – Stream (2.2 mi.)
– Tiorati Circle (6.8 mi.)

Food – Tiorati Circle—in season only (6.8 mi.)

Phone – Tiorati Circle (6.8 mi.)

Camping – Stockbridge Shelter (8.0 mi.)

ACCESS:

To Lake Kanawauke Circle: Via New York State Thruway to exit 15, north on Route 17, northeast on Seven Lakes Drive; via Palisades Interstate Parkway, exit 14, west on former Route 210.   From the circle, go north on Seven Lakes Drive to where the Long Path crosses between Lake Skannatati and Lake Ascoti.

* * * * *

TRAIL DESCRIPTION:

0.0   Follow blazes around north and west shores of lake, then uphill.
2.2   Go left on Dunning Trail (yellow) for 200 yards. Just before it starts to descend, turn right slightly uphill. After crossing stream at Cape Horn, watch for a turn to the right. Trail returns to a very old mine road and crosses notch.
3.0   At Times Square, cross Arden-Surebridge (ASB) Trail (red triangle on white) and Ramapo-Dunderberg Trail (red dot on white), with fireplace nearby. Follow the ASB westward on fire road, shortly turning to the left and leaving the fire road.
3.6   Trailhead on the left of the Lichen Trail (blue L on white).

4.0   White Bar Trail (horizontal blaze) trailhead on left. ASB continues
      ahead. Long Path turns right.
4.8   Cross the Appalachian Trail (Georgia to the left, Maine to the right).
6.8   Cross Arden Valley Road. Lake Tiorati is 0.7 mile to the right (east).
8.0   Stockbridge Shelter with a peaceful view. Two hundred yards further, at
      the foot of a short, steep descent, is the Cave Shelter, sometimes damp.
10.1 Cross Long Mountain Parkway (Route 6) and follow former roadway to
      parking area.

SECTION 7   Long Mountain to Woodbury--Route 32

FEATURE: Brooks Mountain   MAPS: LP Map #4
                                                          TC Map #4
DISTANCE: 11.3 miles   WB Map #6, 8
                                                          HR Map #4
GENERAL DESCRIPTION:

In this section, much of which skirts the boundaries of the U.S. Military
Academy at West Point, the footway is often rough and all of the three climbs
are steep. The second half is largely on paved roads.

FACILITIES:

    Parking   -   Long Mountain Parkway (0.0 mi.)
              -   Route 32, 500 yards south of the railroad trestle (11.3 mi.)

    Water   -   Stream (0.8 mi.)

    Food   -   In both Central Valley & Highland Mills

    Phone   -   In both Central Valley & Highland Mills

    Lodging   -   In both Central Valley & Highland Mills

ACCESS:

Palisades Interstate Parkway, exit 15, west on Route 6 or New York State
Thruway, exit 16, east on Route 6, to parking loop of Long Mountain Parkway
(Route 6), east of Route 293.

                              * * * * *

TRAIL DESCRIPTIONS:

0.0   From parking area on loop of Route 6, go north into the woods.
0.3   Trailheads on the right--Popolopen Gorge Trail (red square on white) and
      Long Mountain Trail (white).
0.8   Go left across stream and uphill along cleared area that marks U.S
      Military Academy (West Point) boundary.
1.8   View over Lake Massawippa, then go down.
2.2   Cross lake outlet and start up Brooks Mountain.
2.9   Viewpoint. Go left.
3.3   Cross Route 293 and zigzag steeply up slope of Blackcap Mountain. The
      footway south is rough.
5.5   Turn right on shoulder of Long Mountain Parkway (Route 6).
6.2   Keep to right of low cable fence and descend an open area to cyclone
      fence. Go through opening and parallel the fence, descending to right to
      Estrada Road (the stub of abandoned Route 6).

7.2   Just past ravine and before (unused) gas pump, turn sharp left down steep
      bank. The path becomes an old road (pre-Revolutionary) and then a gravel
      road.
7.5   Reach Estrada Road, in sight of Thruway, and in 75 yards go right on
      Falkirk Road.
8.3   Go right on Smith Clove Road. Pass golf course.
9.0   Go left on Pine Hill Road over small ridge.
9.3   Pass Skyline Drive on the right, cross Thruway and descend to railway.
9.6   Turn right on gravel road beside remaining single track.
10.1 Turn left off the gravel road, then right on woods road.
11.3 There is a stream between the railroad and Route 32 which may be
      difficult to cross. **DO NOT CROSS THE TRESTLE.** If the water is not too
      high, you may be able to cross at the pipeline. In high water, follow
      the stream downstream (under the trestle) for a few hundred yards until
      it goes under the highway. At this point, climb to the road.

SECTION 8 Woodbury--Route 32 to Salisbury Mills--Route 94

FEATURE: Schunemunk (pronounced Skun-e-munk)

DISTANCE: 9.8 miles

MAPS: LP Map #4
TC Map #8
WB Map #8
HR Map #18

GENERAL DESCRIPTION:

The main feature of this section is the traverse of Schunemunk Mountain, an isolated ridge nearly 1700 ft. above sea level and over eight miles long. Geologically, it is far younger than the Palisades and the Harriman State Park area and is composed of conglomerate overlying shale and sandstone. Most of the mountain is now owned by the Storm King Arts Center, a gift from the Star Expansion Company of Mountainville, which has long welcomed responsible hikers to its property.

West of Clove Road the trail crosses Woodcock Mountain, all on private property, and descends to the Village of Salisbury Mills.

FACILITIES:

Parking – Woodbury, Route 32, 500 ft. south of railroad trestle (0.0 mi.)
– Gravel road off Clove Road (5.6 mi.)
– Salisbury Mills (6.9 mi.) just east of Station Road

Water – Salisbury Mills (6.9 mi.) just east of Station Road

Food – Salisbury Mills (6.9 mi.) just east of Station Road

Phone – Salisbury Mills (6.9 mi.) just east of Station Road

Lodging – None

ACCESS:

New York State Thruway, exit 16, north on Route 32 for four miles. Pick up the Long Path under the railroad trestle.

* * * * *

TRAIL DESCRIPTION:

0.0 From just east of the trestle over Route 32, go steeply up to the quarry road and under the trestle. **Watch out for trucks!** Turn right up to track, then continue north along the tracks.
0.4 Go left on gravel road, angling back.
0.5 At edge of sandpit, trail enters woods on right across a ditch.
0.7 Trail bears sharply right and ascends on a wide footway.
1.3 Little Knob, with views through the oaks. Trail dips slightly, then climbs steeply along western edge of knob, with views to the west.

1.6   High Knob has a bare top with excellent views in all directions.   The
      trail descends to the west and continues along an escarpment with
      occasional pines and continuous views of the main ridge of Schunemunk.

2.5   Cross watercourse, the headwaters of Dark Hollow Brook, but often dry.
      Climb to the ridge.

2.7   Join the Jessup Trail (yellow blazes) which comes in from the left
      (south). Turn right with it to reach a higher ledge and then turn left
      down the long slopes of bare rock, leaving the Jessup Trail.   There are
      two very steep climbs on the lower slope.

3.0   Cross stream flowing left.   In this glen the trail is sometimes obscure,
      but its general direction is up the far side and then to the right.   Soon
      it is on the first of a series of short parallel ridges and makes brief
      descents to cross from one to another as it continues northward.

4.1   Barton Hollow Trail (red) begins on right.   Go left.   The footway becomes
      a gravel road and descends steadily.

4.6   Spring on right.

4.7   Cross brook flowing to left.

4.9   Join another woods road coming from right.   Trail soon becomes wet.

5.5   Turn left on Clove Road at old house.   **No parking here!!**   Also there are
      no blazes southbound at the private owner's request.   Pass Camp Lenni
      Le-na-pe.

5.6   Turn right on gravel road.

5.9   At the T, go left.   Road bears around right uphill.   When it is level,
      watch for trail entering woods on left.

6.2   Trail leaves road to woods on left and makes a wide arc around a corral
      before turning uphill again.

7.5   Woodcock Hill (1030 ft.) has remains of a cable TV tower at viewpoint
      north and east.   The long mountain is Schunemunk; below it in the valley
      to the left, the railroad crosses Moodna Viaduct on a long iron bridge.
      The trail descends the gentle grassy slope, then makes two obscure jogs
      right and descends very steeply and then along shoulder with repeated
      views to the right.

7.7   Join woods road coming from left and descend on it to right.

8.2   Cross abandoned Woodcock Mountain Road into meadow.   The trail enters
      woods on the far side of the meadow high on the slope.

8.6   A horse trail enters from right.

9.0   When horse trail enters open field with views of houses across valley,
      leave it to the right and go to the edge of trees.   Follow edge of field
      along stone wall.

9.2   Pass large cedar with a white house visible ahead.

9.3   Reach Woodcock Mountain Road.   Go to the right-hand edge of the lawn and
      then descend along edge of trees with fenced area to left.

9.4   Go through thin belt of trees onto abandoned railway (Vail's Gate line of
      Erie RR).   Go left.

9.5   After crossing Moodna Creek on iron bridge, turn right along creek bank.

9.7   At Weir's ice cream stand, turn right along highway.

9.8   Station Road begins on left.

SECTION 9   Salisbury Mills--Route 94 to Rock Tavern--Route 207

FEATURE: New York, Ontario & Western Railroad right-of-way

DISTANCE: 7.3 miles

GENERAL DESCRIPTION:

MAPS: LP Map #4, 5
TC Map --
WB Map --
HR Map #60

The beginning of this section is on roads. The trail then turns off and uses the former New York, Ontario & Western Railway bed, now privately owned. Hikers use it by permission of the owners. The terrain through the section is level.

FACILITIES:

> **Parking**   Undesignated, but limited space at:
> - Salisbury Mills (0.0 mi.) just east of Station Road
> - Rock Tavern (7.3 mi.)
>
> **Water**   - Salisbury Mills (0.0 mi.) just east of Station Road
>
> **Food**   - Salisbury Mills (0.0 mi.) just east of Station Road
>
> **Phone**   - Salisbury Mills (0.0 mi.) just east of Station Road
> - Rock Tavern Post Office (6.5 mi.) (then off trail 0.8 mile)
>
> **Lodging** - None

ACCESS:

New York State Thruway, exit 16, west on Route 17 Quickway, north on Route 208, right on Clove Road (Route 27), left in Salisbury Mills to Route 94 at Station Road.

* * * * *

TRAIL DESCRIPTION:

0.0   From Route 94 go north on Station Road through a residential area.
2.1   Continuing on Station Road, pass under the old Erie Railroad.
2.6   Just before a short hill, bear left on an old unpaved road. Pass the foundation of a station and turn left on former roadbed, now widened by landowner to a gravel road. The trail passes a housing development to the left, then beehives on the right. The trail soon becomes overgrown and swampy. In about a mile, the trail reverts to the roadbed.
3.2   Cross Toleman Road.
3.4   Cross Bull Road.
4.7   Cross Shaw Road.
5.4   Cross Beattie Road. Trail becomes a fine gravel road.
6.3   When the gravel road turns left toward a minor paved road, continue straight to Route 207 at Rock Tavern.

7.3 The trail crosses Route 207 between Twin Arch Road and Forrester Road.
     Rock Tavern Post Office is to the right 0.8 mile.

SECTION 10   Rock Tavern—Route 207 to Montgomery—Route 17K

FEATURE: Mainly road walking   **MAPS:**   LP Map #5
                                                          TC Map ––
DISTANCE: 7.2 miles   WB Map ––
                                                          HR Map #60
GENERAL DESCRIPTION:

The Long Path continues on the old railroad bed at the beginning of this
section and then comes out on roads to begin a long stretch of road walking,
passing through the Village of Maybrook.

FACILITIES:

   Parking – At each end and at many intermediate spots along the trail.

   Water   – Maybrook (2.8 mi.)
                – Montgomery (7.2 mi.)

   Food   – Maybrook (2.8 mi.)
                – Montgomery (7.2 mi.)

   Phone   – Maybrook (2.8 mi.)
                – Montgomery (7.2 mi.)

   Lodging – Montgomery (7.2 mi.)

ACCESS:

New York State Thruway, exit 16, west on Route 17 Quickway, north on Route 208,
east on Route 207 to Rock Tavern between Twin Arch Road and Forrester Road.

                           * * * * *

TRAIL DESCRIPTION:

0.0 Descend from Route 207 at the east end of guardrail.
0.3 Cut below powerline is partially blocked with debris of felled trees.
0.4 Overhead is the skeleton of an iron bridge.
1.0 Cross Route 208. (The next section has a clear path, and there are no
     signs posted against trespass. If signs are put up, go right on Route
     208.)
1.4 Turn right on Station Road, passing farms.
1.9 Go left on Route 208.
2.0 Turn right on abandoned Barron Road.
2.6 Former railroad marshalling yards. Continue straight onto Main Street.
     Turn left on Homestead Avenue (Route 208).
2.8 Turn right on Clark Place and ascend. At village boundary, it becomes
     Maybrook Road.
3.8 Turn right on Neeleytown Road, soon entering a grove of trees.
4.0 Take left fork onto Beaverdam Road.

4.8   Interstate 84 goes overhead.

5.8   Pass Chandler Lane on left as farmland gives way to suburbia.

6.3   As Beaverdam Road ends, turn left on Goodwill Road.

6.5   Just over crest of small hill, Goodwill Road turns sharp right while Boyd
      Road goes straight ahead.   Stay on Goodwill.

6.8   Go left on Ward Street (Routes 17K and 211).   When Route 211 goes left,
      stay on Route 17K.

7.1   Turn right on Route 17K on Bridge Street.

7.2   Cross the Wallkill River on highway bridge.

SECTION 11   Montgomery--Route 17K to Ulsterville--Route 52

FEATURE: All roads

DISTANCE: 11.0 miles

MAPS: LP Map #5
TC Map --
WB Map --
HR Map #60

GENERAL DESCRIPTION:

Except for a quarter mile, this section is all on paved roads, largely in a farming area.

FACILITIES:

Parking - Montgomery (0.0 mi.)
- Ulsterville (11.0 mi.)

Water - Montgomery (0.0 mi.)

Food - Montgomery (0.0 mi.)
- Searsville (5.8 mi.)

Phone - Montgomery (0.0 mi.)
- Searsville (5.8 mi.)

Lodging - Montgomery (0.0 mi.)

Camping - Camping is permitted (8.6 mi.) on the property of veteran hikers Mr. & Mrs. Fred Schmelzer, whose home is just across from Box 433-A. There is water from an outside faucet on side of house. If you park, check with them before you leave the car, or leave a note on windshield. No fires are allowed.

ACCESS:

Interstate 84, north on Route 208, west on Route 17K to Montgomery.

* * * * *

TRAIL DESCRIPTION:

0.0 From center of Montgomery, cross the Wallkill River on highway bridge. Road bears left along river. Stay on Route 17K past Mongtomery Road.
0.3 Angle right onto Corbett Road.
2.4 Turn right on Valley Road and in 0.1 mile, left on Winding Hill Road.
4.3 Turn right on Youngblood Road.
5.1 Turn right on Collabar Road.
5.6 Turn right in Searsville on Bullville Road (County Rt. 43).
5.8 Turn left on County Route 17 opposite small store.
6.2 Turn right on Howell Street.
6.8 Go left on Warn Avenue.
7.4 Cross railroad.

7.5 Jog right on Route 302 and descend Bruyn Avenue.

8.2 Cross Gillespie Street.

8.6 Just as the road turns sharply to the left, the Long Path enters the field straight ahead and parallels Shawangunk Kill. (Camping behind house on left.) After a tree-girt meadow, the trail runs along the bank for 0.7 mile. Keep out of hay and corn.

9.3 Cross creek on narrow road bridge and go up hill.

9.5 Go right on Route 55.

9.8 Turn left to cottage colony around Pinecliff Lake (no swimming!).

11.0 Reach Route 52 (Ulsterville).

SECTION 12   Ulsterville to Route 44-55/Jenny Lane

FEATURE: Shawangunks

DISTANCE: 16.5 miles

MAPS: LP Map #5
TC Map #9
WB Map #9, 10
HR Map #41A, 65

GENERAL DESCRIPTION:

After the first five miles--much of it on roads, the trail enters the woods and climbs above Verkeerder Kill Falls to cross the Shawangunks through Minnewaska State Park. The mountain (called Shon-gums or "Gunks") is characterized by steep slopes used in some areas for rock climbing, and gently rolling plateaus. Its three lakes are all beautiful; Awosting is in the State Park, and Minnewaska and Mohonk are currently on private land. As of this date, the State is planning to acquire the property surrounding Lake Minnewaska and add it to Minnewaska State Park. Please check with the Palisades Interstate Park Commission (914/786-2701; 212/562-8688) to see if the State has already acquired this property.

FACILITIES:

Parking - Ulsterville (0.0 mi.)
         - Daschner's, by special arrangement* (5.0 mi.)
         - Route 44-55, state parking area (15.7 mi.)
         - Jenny Lane (16.5 mi.)

*Mr. and Mrs. Daschner on Upper Mountain Road permit hikers to park on their property. Their house is on the left, with a fieldstone front behind thick trees. Just beyond the house, a narrow drive leads uphill over a hump to a wide, cleared area out of sight of the road. Before you start up the trail, tell Mrs. Daschner that your car is there and when you expect to return to it. **Do not park anywhere else on this road**. It is very narrow and has no shoulders. The few pulloffs that have been made are private areas for local residents. Do not block the Daschner driveway, nor any other road, drive, or lane--not even a woods road. **As we go to press, the Daschners are in the process of selling their house and land. Access may change. Please respect private property. For up-to-date information, call the Trail Conference (212/696-6800).**

Water - Several streams (some seasonal)

Food - None

Phone - 0.7 miles east on Rt. 44-55 at entrance to Lake Minnewaska

Lodging - None

ACCESS:

Interstate 84, north on Route 208, west on Route 52 to Ulsterville.

TRAIL DESCRIPTION:

0.0 From the corner of Lake Shore Road and Route 52 in Ulsterville, jog right on the highway and then left on Quanacutt Road, briefly uphill. The road passes between stone pillars and crosses a brook. Then it becomes a woods road. At paved Registro Road, turn right.

3.2 Reach Crawford and go right on Turnpike Road, then immediately left on Church Road, at first parallel to Verkeeder Kill.

3.5 Go left on Upper Mountain Road (Daschner Road).

5.0 The Daschner home is on the left **(see note under "Parking")**.

5.1 Start uphill on blue-blazed trail.

6.1 Prospect Rock. The rim trail joins from below left. Just beyond is Fall View Lookout below Verkeerder Kill Falls (Katykill Falls).

6.3 Go left a way from old trail, following blazes. (Do not use the former Peter Buck Trail that passes Mud Pond on the east. The landowner has closed this section.)

6.4 Lookout Rock on top of the escarpment.

6.5 Turn right. Do not follow the former route to left; it goes onto private land of Ice Caves.

7.4 Cross outlet of Mud Pond in Minnewaska State Park.

8.3 Reach Lake Awosting and turn right. In 60 yards the blue blazes of the Long Path go to the right, up an old carriage road on the route of the former Scenic Trail. (The former route of the LP continues on the gravel road along the east shore of the lake, passing the bathing beach which is open only in summer and when a lifeguard is on duty. It is 2.3 miles to the causeway over Fly Brook. If speed is essential, turn left on the shore road--it is 0.3 mi shorter along the west bank with less change of elevation; this road passes the ranger cabin.)
The Long Path's present route follows the Scenic Trail, whose yellow blazes may still be found along with the LP blazes. It is 5.1 miles to the causeway with several very steep descents and three short, very steep climbs. There are a number of very fine views, a 20-yard natural tunnel, and the base of Rainbow Falls, a cooling spot.

8.7 Reach the first viewpoint on Murray Hill. The road ends in another 0.1 mi. at a fine viewpoint east toward the Hudson Valley. The LP becomes a footpath and in another 0.1 mi. rises to a knob with a 360 degree view: Lake Awosting is to the west, the distant Catskill Mountains to the west and north, and the Hudson Valley to the east.

9.0 About 80 yards downhill, go left on an overgrown path through Spruce Glen.

9.3 Turn right on an old carriage road, and in about 80 yards go up left off the road. The LP now runs along the upper edge of Margaret Cliff, with some views.

9.8 Begin descent, at first gentle, then extremely steep and somewhat damp.

10.2 Cross an old carriage road and then a brook; start ascent.

10.3 Natural tunnel. The trail ducks into a cave*--a flashlight is not needed--for 10 yards (take off your pack . . . you and it won't fit together) then comes out in a cleft in which you can stand. Turn right and continue on the Long Path. *For you non-spelunkers, continue on past this cave entrance for 15 feet and rejoin the Long Path. The trail then ascends very steeply.

10.4 On wide, wooded ledge, trail ascends gently toward the upper cliffs.

10.7 Turn right on a carriage road, toward Hamilton Point.

10.9 Reach a carriage road on top of Castle Point with fine view south and east. Descend the winding road toward the left.

11.4 Just after road makes 180 degree left turn, watch closely for hidden trail up to the right into woods. The trail descends the long series of Litchfield Ledges, open bare rock alternating with short wooded sections, often marked with cairns and sometimes very narrow.

12.0 The trail descends extremely steeply for some distance down into Huntington Ravine.

12.1 Turn right on a carriage road (Awosting Road) in a thick forest.

12.5 Turn sharp left downhill on trail.

12.9 After crossing a small brook, the trail reaches the base of Rainbow Falls, which drop over a sheer cliff. From the falls, the trail returns to the floor of the ravine for a few hundred yards before climbing very steeply to the top of the cliff.

13.0 Viewpoint east over ravine and ledges, and shortly after, another viewpoint west.

13.2 Cross brook on a log, then follow cairns and blazes along sloping bedrock.

13.4 Turn right on access road to Lake Awosting. Cross embankment over Fly Brook; the LP turns left here. The road right leads to parking area in 2.3 miles.

16.3 Cross Route 44-55.

16.5 Parking area is on old Wawarsing Turnpike. The trail continues on the gravel road.

SECTION 13   Jenny Lane to Catskill Park--Riggsville

FEATURE: All roads	**MAPS:** LP Map #5, 6
	TC Map #9
DISTANCE: 13.5 miles	WB Map #10, 11
	HR Map #41A, 61

GENERAL DESCRIPTION:

This section is all on roads, connecting the Shawangunks and the Catskills. Almost mid-way is the town of Kerhonkson.

FACILITIES:

> **Parking** ‑ Jenny Lane (0.0 mi.)
>   ‑ End of Shawangunk Drive, limited (1.1 mi.)
>   ‑ Kerhonkson (4.9 mi.)
>
> **Water**   ‑ Route 44-55 (2.8 mi.)
>   ‑ Clay Hill Road (5.1 mi.)
>   ‑ Pataukunk Road (6.6 mi.)
>   ‑ Lower Cherrytown Road (6.8 mi.)
>
> **Food**   ‑ Route 44-55 (2.8 mi.)
>   ‑ Clay Hill Road (5.1 mi.)
>   ‑ Pataukunk Road (6.6 mi.)
>   ‑ Lower Cherrytown Road (6.8 mi.)
>
> **Phone**   ‑ Route 44-55 (2.8 mi.)
>   ‑ Clay Hill Road (5.1 mi.)
>   ‑ Pataukunk Road (6.6 mi.)
>   ‑ Lower Cherrytown Road (6.8 mi.)
>
> **Lodging** ‑ Kerhonkson (4.9 mi.)

ACCESS:

New York State Thruway, exit 18, west on Route 299, west on Route 44-55. Jenny Lane is tricky to find as there is no longer a sign for it. It is off Route 44-55, 4.7 miles west of the junction of Routes 44-55 and 299, and 1.1 mile west of the entrance to Lake Minnewaska on the north side of the road.

* * * * *

TRAIL DESCRIPTION:

0.0 From Jenny Lane north of Route 44-55, go west (left) and pass outlet road to highway; then descend fire road (closed to vehicles).

1.5 Come to the end of Shawangunk Drive (limited parking). There is a pipe spring at the bridge just ahead on the left opposite the house. Continue ahead on the gravel road.

2.3   Continue to County Route 27 (Upper Granit Road) as Shawangunk Drive joins it. Bear left.
2.8   Turn right downhill on Route 44-55.
3.3   Pass road to Granit on the right. Continue on Route 44-55.
3.9   Turn right on road without a sign or route number which will then bear left downhill.
4.9   Reach the town of Kerhonkson. Cross Roundout Creek on road bridge.
5.1   Cross Route 209 straight ahead onto Clay Hill Road.
6.6   Join Pataukunk Road (County Route 3) coming from the right.
6.8   Turn left uphill on Lower Cherrytown Road.
10.4 Turn left between farm buildings on Upper Cherrytown Road.
13.5 Reach start of state trail on the left; parking is in the clearing to the right.

SECTION 14   Catskill Park--Riggsville to Bull Run

FEATURE: Bangle Hill	**MAPS:** LP Map #6
	TC Map #43
DISTANCE: 8.7 miles	WB Map #11
	HR Map #61

GENERAL DESCRIPTION:

At this point, the Long Path enters the Catskill Forest Preserve.   In this section, which is all in the woods, it passes Vernooykill Cascade, and includes the climbs of Samson Mountain and Bangle Hill, plus the steep descent to Bull Run.

Until this point, the Long Path has been maintained by member clubs of the New York-New Jersey Trail Conference and the blazes are painted aqua/blue.   Within the park, most of the trails are maintained by the New York State Department of Environmental Conservation (DEC).   The AMC-Catskill Chapter and Catskill 3500 Clubs do maintain the Long Path from Vernoy Cascade to Gulf Road, and from Gulf Road to the Denning Lean-to, respectively.

Different colored markers are used to indicate the various trails within the park trail system.   The route of the Long Path follows DEC trails; therefore, the color of the blazes will change as the route connects from one trail to the next.   The blue painted Conference blazes continue up to Gulf Road at the end of Section 14.   **Beware at trail junctions and turns indicated in the Guide. Even though most trail junctions are now marked with Trail Conference Long Path markers, the only way to be sure you are following the Long Path is to follow the Guide carefully and note the color of the markers to be followed.**   At trail junctions when a different color blaze will be followed, the color will be written in the text in CAPS.

FACILITIES:

>   **Parking** - Upper Cherrytown Road (0.0 mi.)
>   - Sundown-West Shokan Rd., also known as Gulf Road and Peeka-
>   moose Road (8.7 mi.)
>
>   **Water** - Vernooykill Cascade (1.8 mi.)
>   - Intermittently along the trail.
>   - Sundown Primitive Campground (8.7 mi.)
>
>   **Food** - None
>
>   **Phone** - None
>
>   **Camping** - Overnight site--Sundown Primitive Campground (8.7 mi.).

Camping is permitted on state land below 3500 ft. provided the campsite is at least 150 ft. from trail and from water.   Fires must be on rock or thoroughly cleared land and be completely out (cool enough for your hand!) before departure.   Stoves are much to be preferred.

Litter should not be buried! (Animals will dig it up.) Everything you carry in should be carried out. Human waste should be buried at least 150 ft. from water, trail, or campsite.

DO NOT CUT LIVING TREES FOR ANY REASON WHATEVER!!!

ACCESS:

New York State Thruway, exit 18, west on Route 299, west on Route 44-55. Follow the trail description in Section 13 from Route 44-55 (2.8 mi.) to the end of the section.

* * * * *

TRAIL DESCRIPTION:

0.0 From Upper Cherrytown Road, follow the RED trail into the woods.
1.8 Vernooykill Cascade to the left. Turn sharp right uphill on gravel road then left onto trail on slope of Pople Hill. When the Long Path leaves an established DEC trail, our standard blue blazes will be found. Turn left at gravel road, which continues to Greenville. Watch for turnoff uphill to right on footpath. This continues around shoulder of Sampson Mountain, over Bangle Hill (2350 ft.) and very steeply downward.
8.7 Gulf Road (Peekamoose Road). This leads to Sundown to the left and West Shokan to the right. The state primitive campground (no facilities) is to the left along the stream.

SECTION 15   Bull Run to Denning Road

FEATURE: Peekamoose & Table Mountain   **MAPS:**   LP Map #6
                                                                TC Map #43
DISTANCE: 7.5 miles   WB Map #11
                                                                HR Map #61, 66
GENERAL DESCRIPTION:

A strenuous section, the trail goes over Peekamoose and Table Mountains, both
of which have wooded summits. The trail in this section is marked in blue.
The color of the blazes is noted in the text in CAPS when there is a change.

FACILITIES:

    Parking – Gulf Road; also known as Sundown-West Shokan Road and Peeka-
             moose Road (0.0 mi.)
            – Denning Road, 1.1 mi. from the Long Path, at the end of the
             gravel road from Claryville (7.5 mi.)

    Water – Sundown Primitive Campground on Sundown-West Shokan Road. There
             is no sign; it is just west of the trail crossing. No fee (0.0
             mi.)
            – Denning Lean-to (7.3 mi.)

    Food – None

    Phone – None

    Camping – Sundown Primitive Campground on Sundown-West Shokan Road. There
             is no sign; it is just west of the trail crossing. No fee (0.0
             mi.)
            – Denning Lean-to (7.3 mi.)

ACCESS:

New York State Thruway, exit 19, west on Route 28, south on Route 28A, west on
Sundown-West Shokan Road, also known as Gulf Road and Peekamoose Road.

* * * * *

TRAIL DESCRIPTION:

0.0   From the base of Bangle Hill, go north (toward Shokan) on Gulf Road/
       Sundown-West Shokan Road.
0.5   Turn left just before the state parking lot and go uphill on old woods
       road.
1.7   Turn right off road; go steeply uphill along ridge.
3.5   Reconnoiter Rock to right: Good views
3.7   On the right, pass red-blazed trail which leads back to Gulf Road. Pass
       spring on the left.

4.4   Reach the summit of Peekamoose Mountain (3843 ft.) with no view. The
      ascent and the descent of this peak are steep. The trail alternates
      between rocky and steep, and a more reasonable grade.
4.7   Saddle between mountains.
5.4   Reach the wooded summit of Table Mountain (3847 ft.). On a tree, above
      eye level, find a small metal register box maintained by the Catskill
      3500 Club.
5.7   Small spring on right of trail.
7.3   Cross Neversink Creek on a split log (this is slippery in wet weather;
      depending on the water level, the creek can be forded a little farther
      downstream). Denning Lean-to is on the opposite bank. The trail from
      the lean-to up to the yellow-blazed trail (0.25 mile) is marked with blue
      blazes as well as occasional red blazes.
7.5   Reach Old Denning Road at the junction with the YELLOW-blazed Phoenicia-
      East Branch Trail. (To the left it is 1.15 mi. to the parking area at
      the end of the gravel road from Claryville.) The Long Path turns right.

SECTION 16   Old Denning Road to Woodland Valley

FEATURE: Slide, Cornell, and Wittenberg Mountains   **MAPS:**   LP Map #6
                                                                           TC Map #43
DISTANCE: 11.1 miles   WB Map #11, 12
                                                                           HR Map #66

GENERAL DESCRIPTION:

This section of the trail is rugged, rocky, and steep in some parts, but the
views from the peaks are worth the climb. The trail in this section is marked
in yellow, blue, and red. The color of the trail marker to be followed is
noted in the text in CAPS where a change in trails occurs.

FACILITIES:

    Parking – Denning Road (County Road 19), 1.1 mi. from the Long Path at
                the end of the gravel road from Claryville (0.0 mi.)
           – Woodland Valley Public Campsite, fee charged (11.1 mi.)

    Water   – Spring (1.5 mi.)
             – Spring north of Slide Mountain (4.3 mi.)
             – Terrace Lean-to (8.6 mi.) .9 mile off the trail
             – Woodland Valley (11.1 mi.)

    Food   – None

    Phone   – Woodland Valley Public Campsite (11.1 mi.)

    Lodging – Phoenicia (16.5 mi.)

    Camping – Terrace Lean-to (8.6 mi.) .9 mile off the trail
               – Woodland Valley Public Campsite, fee charged (11.1 mi.)

ACCESS:

New York State Thruway Exit 16. Take Route 17 west 54 miles to Liberty (exit
100). At end of exit ramp, turn left and go to first traffic light. Turn left
onto Route 52 west. Go one mile and turn right onto Route 55 east. Go ten
miles to Curry. Look for sign on right marked "Claryville." Turn left onto
County Road 19 (Denning Road) and continue for 14 miles until the road ends.
At four miles you will pass County Road 47 on the left, which leads to Frost
Valley.

OR . . .

New York State Thruway exit 18, west on Route 299, west on Route 44-55 to
Curry; turn right onto County Road 19 (Denning Road) as described above.

* * * * *

TRAIL DESCRIPTION:

0.0   At the intersection of the blue/red trail coming from the Denning Lean-to and the YELLOW-marked Phoenicia-East Branch Trail, turn right; the trail follows an old road. Coming from Denning Road, continue straight.

1.5   Spring located on the left.

1.8   Turn right onto BLUE-blazed Curtis Trail. (The yellow trail leads ahead to Winisook Lake.) The BLUE-blazed trail ascends gradually, then more steeply.

2.5   Flat rock ledge and lookout to the right of trail. View toward Lone, Table, and Rocky Mountains.

3.4   Turn right onto RED-marked Wittenberg-Cornell-Slide Trail. (To the left, the red trail meets the yellow trail and goes to Winnisook Lake.) The red trail is at first a wide jeep road, becoming more rugged as it ascends. Approaching the summit, this trail ascends gradually onto a woods road.

4.1   Reach the summit of Slide Mountain (4180 ft.), the highest peak in the Catskills. Here there is a large boulder with a plaque dedicated to John Burroughs, a Catskill native and naturalist, a poet of nature. Camping and fires are not permitted on the summit. Begin steep descent heading eastward. Not far below the summit, you will come to a spring on your left.

5.0   Come to a col, the lowest point between Cornell and Slide Mountains. There is a spring a short distance to the right.

6.0   A seasonal spring is located on the left.

6.5   The yellow spur trail to the right goes 0.1 mi. to the summit of Cornell Mountain (3860 ft.). Descend steeply to the col between Cornell and Wittenberg Mountains.

7.3   Reach the summit of Wittenberg Mountain (3780 ft.), providing an excellent view over the Ashokan Reservoir. Begin the descent, with alternately steep and moderate grades. Pass rock overhang on the left not far below the summit.

7.5   Pass seasonal spring on the left.

8.6   The Long Path turns left. The yellow spur trail ahead leads 0.9 mi down to the Terrace Mountain Lean-to.

11.1 Reach Woodland Valley Public Campsite. The trail passes a campsite before reaching Woodland Valley Road. Turn left to register for a campsite. The Long Path turns right onto the road.

SECTION 17   Woodland Valley to Phoenicia

FEATURE: All roads; crosses Esopus Creek   **MAPS:**   LP Map #6
                                                                      TC Map #42, 41
DISTANCE: 6.3 miles   WB Map #12, 13
                                                                      HR Map #66
GENERAL DESCRIPTION:

This is a fairly scenic road walk from the base of Wittenberg Mountain into the
Town of Phoenicia. There are few markers along the route.

FACILITIES:

    Parking – Woodland Valley Public Campsite, fee charged (0.0 mi.)
              – Phoenicia (6.3 mi.)

    Water – Woodland Valley (0.0 mi.)
           – Phoenicia (6.3 mi.)

    Food – Phoenicia (6.3 mi.)

    Phone – Woodland Valley (0.0 mi.)
           – Phoenicia (6.3 mi.)

    Lodging – Phoenicia (6.3 mi.)

    Camping – Woodland Valley Public Campsite, fee charged (0.0 mi.)

ACCESS:

New York State Thruway, exit 19, west on Route 28 to Phoenicia, south on
Woodland Valley Road 5 miles to Woodland Valley Public Campsite.

* * * * *

TRAIL DESCRIPTION:

0.0 At Woodland Valley Campsite, go east along the Woodland Valley Road (from
     the descent of Wittenberg Mountain, turn right). There are few markers
     along this section.
4.4 Cross stream.
5.5 Cross Esopus Creek.
5.7 Turn right onto Route 28; turn left on Route 214 and continue straight
     ahead into Phoenicia (do not follow Route 214).
6.3 Reach the center of Phoenicia.

SECTION 18   Phoenicia to Lake Hill--Route 212

FEATURE: Mount Tremper

DISTANCE: 11.6 miles

MAPS: LP Map #7A
TC Map #41
WB Map #13
HR Map #66, 25

GENERAL DESCRIPTION:

The trail is on roads at the beginning and end of this section. In between, it makes the steep climb over Mount Tremper. The trail is blazed in red and blue in this section. The color of the blazes is noted in the text in CAPS when there is a change in trails.

FACILITIES:

Parking — Phoenicia (0.0 mi.)
         — Route 40 near the trailhead (1.4 mi.)
         — Willow (9.0 mi.)
         — Lake Hill (11.6 mi.)

Water   — Phoenicia (0.0 mi.)
         — Spring (2.3 mi.)
         — Spring (3.4 mi.)

Food   — Phoenicia (0.0 mi.)

Phone   — Willow Post Office (9.2 mi.)

Lodging — Phoenicia (0.0 mi.)

ACCESS:

New York State Thruway, exit 19, west on Route 28, north at sign to Phoenicia.

* * * * *

TRAIL DESCRIPTION:

0.0 From the center of Phoenicia, go south on County Route 40 (old Route 28), which is on the east side of the Esopus Creek.
1.4 Turn left off the road and climb steep uphill on RED-marked Phoenicia-Mt. Tremper Trail.
2.3 Pass a spring on the left.
3.2 Reach the Baldwin Memorial Lean-to.
3.2 Pass a pipe spring, 50 ft. left of the trail.
4.1 Reach old Mount Tremper Lean-to.
4.2 Reach the summit of Mount Tremper (2740 ft.), where there is a fire tower no longer being used. The red trail ends here and the BLUE-marked Willow Trail begins. Follow the blue markers.
7.6 The trail leaves the ridge, going down to the right, and becomes a gravel road.

8.0 The gravel road becomes paved Jessup Road, where houses begin. There is no space to park here.

9.0 Willow crossroads and post office. Continue on paved road.

9.3 Turn left onto Route 212. For the most part, there are no markers along this road.

11.6 Reach Mink Hollow Road in Lake Hill.

SECTION 19   Lake Hill—Route 212 to Platte Clove Road

FEATURE: Devil's Path

DISTANCE: 13.0 miles

GENERAL DESCRIPTION:

The Long Path continues along the rugged terrain of the Catskills.   This section abounds with beautiful scenery and impressive views, and crosses Sugarloaf (3800 ft.) and Twin (3640 ft.) Mountain.   The trail in this section is blazed in blue, red, blue, and red again.   The color of the blazes is noted in the text in CAPS when there is a change in trails.

FACILITIES:

Parking	–	Lake Hill (0.0 mi.)
	–	Mink Hollow Road (3.0 mi.)
	–	Parking area, limited (11.9 mi.)
Water	–	Mink Hollow Lean-to (5.9 mi.)
	–	Spring (6.4 mi.)
Food	–	None
Phone	–	None
Lodging	–	None
Camping	–	Mink Hollow Lean-to (5.9mi.)

ACCESS:

New York State Thruway, exit 20, west on Route 212 to Lake Hill.

* * * * *

TRAIL DESCRIPTIONS:

0.0   From the corner of Route 212 go north on the BLUE-blazed Mink Hollow Trail on Mink Hollow Road, which is drivable for 3 miles although the last 0.2 mi. is very rough.   Along the road, blazes are found mostly on telephone poles.   Pass a farm and creek.

2.9   Pass driveway on the left; the trail goes to the right.   Pass register box. The road becomes rough.

3.0   Pass ruins of an old mill on your right.   (Space to park here.)   Turn left onto gravel road; cross creek.

4.6   Cross creek; continue on woods road.

5.9   Reach the Mink Hollow Lean-to on the left.   The blue trail continues ahead to Platte Clove Road.   The Long Path turns right uphill and follows the RED-blazed trail, Devil's Path.   The red trail to the left leads to Plateau,

Hunter, and West Kill Mountains. This is also the divide between the Esopus and Schoharie Creeks. FOLLOW THE RED TRAIL TO THE RIGHT.

6.4 Pass spring on the right.
6.8 Reach the summit of Sugarloaf Mountain (3800 ft.).
8.0 Pecoy Notch. The blue trail to the left heads down to Platte Clove Road.
8.6 Summit of Twin Mountain (3640 ft.).
9.2 East peak of Twin Mountain. Great views.
9.7 Jimmy Dolan Notch. Turn left on the Jimmy Dolan Trail, following BLUE markers. Descend steeply. (The red-blazed Devil's Path continues over Indian Head Mountain.)
11.3 Cross Schoharie Creek and reach the junction with the Devil's Path (red markers) coming in from the right. Turn left, following RED markers.
11.9 Come to a very small parking area and follow Prediger Road northward.
12.3 Turn right on Platte Clove Road. Pass NYC Police Camp and descend.
13.3 Just after passing a white house and barn with lawns on both sides of the road, the section ends at the gravel road on the left, a marked snowmobile trail.

SECTION 20   Platte Clove Road to Palenville

FEATURE: **MAPS:**   LP Map #7A
                                                            TC Map #41
DISTANCE: miles   WB Map #13
                                                            HR Map #71, 35
GENERAL DESCRIPTION:

FACILITIES:

    Parking

    Water

    Food

    Phone

    Lodging

ACCESS:

* * * * *

TRAIL DESCRIPTION:

Permission has been received from the New York State Department of Environmental Conservation to complete the remaining open section of the Long Path.

Construction is under way and this section should be open in the spring of 1987.

If you would like us to send you this update when the section is completed, please send a stamped, self-addressed envelope to the Trail Conference office.

* * * * *

TRAIL DESCRIPTION:

0.0   Turn left off Platte Clove Mountain Road and follow
      snowmobile trail uphill on an old road. Follow blue-blazes.
0.7   Turn right onto another dirt road.
1.0   Turn right off Old Steamberg Road and follow another old
      woods road north.
1.1   Intersect unofficial trail, marked with faded red markers,
      that leads right to Huckleberry Point. Continue straight
      ahead on nearly level grades.
1.4   Cross a pair of streams in a swampy area. After the second
      crossing, the ascent, often steep, resumes as the trail
      climbs to the north flank of Kaaterskill High Peak at 3,000
      feet elevation.
2.3   Begin crossing Pine Plains, the highest point reached on
      High Peak. The trail continues through swampy terrain. The
      forest for the next 3/4 mile is typical of higher elevations
      with considerable spruce, hemlock and birch.
3.5   The snowmobile trail (yellow or red) turns left uphill,
      (the start of the snowmobile trail loop is roughly 0.1 mile
      further on) while the Long Path follows blue blazes straight
      ahead. The trail soon begins to descend through drier
      terrain.
3.7   Turn right (north) on old Twilight Park Trail and descend
      off ridge. The descent is steep and contains many small
      switchbacks. (Turn left here to bushwhack 3/4 miles to
      Kaaterskill High Peak.)
4.2   Leave old trail and begin to descend steeply through a
      series of sharp slopes and narrow flat ledges.
4.8   The trail reaches another narrow ledge, turns right on the
      Red Gravel Hill Road, and begins to run along the edge of
      the great drop to Kaaterskill Clove on the left.
5.0   Buttermilk Falls, a spectacular two step waterfall in a great
      ampitheatre. Cross stream and continue along level ledge.
5.5   Wildcat Falls. Spectacular waterfall; the ledge on the west
      side has a stunning view of Kaaterskill Clove and the Hudson
      Valley to the east. Cross the stream, continue east, descend
      a small ledge to the left, pass a large boulder, and bear
      right along the slope edge again.
6.4   Cross the two streams of Hillyer Ravine. This is the last
      sure water. Continue, nearly level, crossing several
      intermittent streams.
7.0   Pass over break in slope and begin to descend. The trail is
      downhill, often steep, until reaching Malden Avenue. The
      trail uses several long switchbacks in its descent. An old
      bluestone quarry is passed on the right.
8.5   Cross border of state land. Trail markers change from blue-
      discs to turquoise blazes. The trail soon bears left onto a
      woods road.
9.0   Reach Malden Avenue-Palenville and turn left along pavement.
9.5   Route 23A and Malden Avenue in Palenville. Turn right.
9.9   Section ends just east of a Catskill Forest Preserve sign at
      the beginning of the Sleepy Hollow Horse Trail.

SECTION 20   Platte Clove Road to Palenville

		MAPS:	LP Map #7A

FEATURE: Kaaterskill High Peak

MAPS: LP Map #7A
TC Map #41
DISTANCE: 9.9 miles
WB Map #13
HR Map #71

GENERAL DESCRIPTION:

This section of the Long Path follows the High Peak Snowmobile Trail around the eastern and northern flanks of Kaaterskill High Peak for the first 3 1/2 miles. North of High peak it descends to follow the remnants of the Red Gravel Hill Road into Palenville. Along this old road the trail passes a number of beautiful waterfalls. The Long Path follows blue-discs most of the way, except at the Palenville end where it is marked with turquoise paint rectangles. Parking, of unknown legality, is available on the south side of Platte Clove Mountain Road about 100 feet east of the trail head. Parking, again of unknown legality, may be found on the north side of Malden Avenue about 100 feet beyond where the trail joins this road.

FACILITIES:

Parking – Platte Clove Road (0.0 mi.)
         – Palenville – Route 23A (9.5 mi.)

Water   – Stream crossing (1.4 mi.)
         – Buttermilk Falls (5.0 mi.)
         – Wildcat Ravine (5.5 mi.)
         – Hillyer Ravine (6.0 mi.)

Food   – Palenville (9.9 mi.)

Phone   – Palenville (9.9 mi.)

Lodging – Palenville (9.9 mi.)

ACCESS:

New York State Thruway to Exit 20, west on Route 212 to Centerville, north on Ulster Route 35, west on Ulster Route 33 to West Saugerties, west on Platte Clove Mountain Road to Devil's Kitchen. <u>Winter route</u> – New York State Thruway to Exit 20, north on Route 32 to Route 32A, north on Route 32A to Palenville, west on Route 23A to Tannersville, south and east on Greene Route 16 (Platte Clove Mountain Road) to Devil's Kitchen.

SECTION 21 Palenville--Route 23A to North Lake

FEATURE: North Lake   MAPS: LP Map #7B
                                                        TC Map #40, 41
DISTANCE: 5.5 miles   WB Map #13
                                                        HR Map #35, 71

GENERAL DESCRIPTION:

At the beginning of the section, the Long Path picks up part of a horse trail
which leads to the Escarpment Trail, which the Long Path follows to its
northern terminus. The grades in this section are fairly moderate and there are
several viewpoints from the escarpment over the Hudson Valley. The trail in
this section is blazed in yellow and blue. The color of the blazes is noted in
the text in CAPS when there is a change in trails.

FACILITIES:

     Parking - Palenville (0.0 mi.)
              - Route 23A, various available parking areas
              - North Lake Public Campsite, fee charged (5.5 mi.)

     Water   - Palenville (0.0 mi.)
              - North Lake (5.5 mi.)

     Food   - Palenville (0.0 mi.)

     Phone   - Palenville (0.0 mi.)
              - North Lake Public Campsite (5.5 mi.)

     Lodging - Palenville (0.0 mi.)

     Camping - North Lake Public Campsite, fee charged (5.5 mi.)

ACCESS:

New York State Thruway, exit 20, north on Route 32, west on Route 32A and then
west on Route 23A; or New York State Thruway, exit 21, west on Route 23, south
on Route 32, west on Route 23A to Palenville.

                         * * * * *

TRAIL DESCRIPTION:

0.0 The trail begins west of Palenville just before the sign "Catskill Park,"
     0.8 mile below the bridge at Malden Avenue. The trail, a former
     carriage road and now a bridle path, is part of the Sleepy Hollow Horse
     Trail network. It is marked with YELLOW blazes and follows a steady
     grade uphill. Woods road comes in on the right.

Pass register; please sign in. Pass shallow spring on the right.

3.2   The horse trail (yellow blazes) on the right leads to Rip Van Winkle
      Rest. Continue ahead to the Escarpment Trail.

3.3   Reach the junction with the BLUE-blazed Escarpment Trail, which the Long
      Path follows to its northern terminus at Windham. Turn right and follow
      the blue markers . The blue trail to the left leads to Inspiration Point
      and Sunset Rock, affording scenic views over the Hudson Valley.

3.8   Reach the junction with the red trail which goes left to the site of the
      Kaaterskill Hotel. Turn right and follow blue blazes along flat grassy
      trail.

4.4   Junction with red trail to the left, a short-cut that avoids Boulder Rock
      and meets the blue trail further up. Turn right and follow blue blazes.

4.6   Boulder Rock, a massive rock sitting near a lookout point. Here there
      are excellent views of Platte Clove and the Hudson Valley.

4.8   The trail ascends before it reaches the junction with red-blazed
      short-cut trail. The trail becomes more rugged and descends.

5.2   Site of the Catskill Mountain House, which was burned in 1963 after it
      had fallen into a dangerous condition of decay. Until 1918, it had been
      possible to reach the site by the Otis Elevator, a funicular railway up
      the east face, the scar of its route being still visible. (See the
      historical marker at the site.) The trail passes through the parking
      area to the left.

5.5   North Lake Road at North Lake Public Campsite, operated by New York State
      Department of Environmental Conservation. North Lake and South Lake were
      once separate with a road crossing between them. They are now a single
      lake. Water, swimming in season, and camping facilities are available
      here.

SECTION 22   North Lake to Batavia Kill

FEATURE:	Blackhead Mountain	**MAPS:** LP Map #7B, 8

MAPS: LP Map #7B, 8
TC Map #41
WB Map #13
HR Map #71, 63

DISTANCE: 11.2 miles

GENERAL DESCRIPTION:

The Long Path in this section continues on the blue-blazed Escarpment Trail, affording fine views over the Hudson Valley. The trail is rugged and in some parts, steep. **Carry an ample supply of water as water sources are only available at Dutcher Notch (0.3 mi. off the trail) or at each end of the section.** The section begins at North Lake, operated by the New York State Department of Environmental Conservation (DEC).

FACILITIES:

Parking – North Lake Public Campsite, fee charged (0.0 mi.)
– Big Hollow Road, 1.5 mi. from the junction of the Long Path and the Batavia Kill Trail

Water – North Lake Public Campsite (0.0 mi.)
– Dutcher Notch, 0.3 mi. on Dutcher Notch Trail (7.9 mi.)
– Batavia Kill Lean-to, 0.2 mi. on Batavia Kill Trail (11.2 mi.)

Food – Haines Falls (3 miles off trail)

Phone – North Lake Public Campsite (0.0 mi.)

Lodging – Haines Falls (3 miles off trail)

Camping – North Lake Public Campsite, fee charged (0.0 mi.)
– Batavia Kill Lean-to, 0.2 mi. on Batavia Kill Trail (11.2 mi.)

ACCESS:

New York State Thruway, exit 20, north on Route 32, west on Route 32A, then Route 23A to Haines Falls; turn north, follow the sign for North Lake.

* * * * *

TRAIL DESCRIPTION:

0.0   The trail is east of the end of the lake; a DEC bulletin board with a topo map is at the trailhead. After passing picnic tables, the trail goes to the right and soon reaches a short, steep climb on a rock ledge.
0.3   Artist's Rock, and the view over the Hudson Valley made famous by Thomas Cole. The trail ascends steeply. Pass yellow-marked trail to the right leading to Sunset Rock.

0.9   Newman's Ledge, also providing excellent views over the Hudson Valley.
      Continue on past Sleepy Hollow Notch; turn left and ascend (do not go
      through the notch).
1.8   Badman's Cave, a natural foundation providing partial shelter. The
      yellow-marked trail left goes to Mary's Glen and Scutt Road. It also
      meets the red-marked trail leading back to North Lake. Follow BLUE
      markers going right and ascend past the cave.
1.9   Find U.S. Geodetic Survey marker on open ledge with views of the valley.
2.4   The red trail to the left leads to Mary's Glen and North Lake Campground
      (1.4 mi.). Follow BLUE blazes to the right and ascend steeply.
2.6   North Point with its view to North Lake.
3.0   North Mountain (3180 ft.). The trail continues through the woods over
      fairly level terrain.
5.6   After an ascent, reach Stoppel Point (3420 ft.). Begin moderate descent.
      Site of an airplane that crashed in 1985 only 10 feet off the trail.
7.9   Dutcher Notch. Yellow-blazed Dutcher Notch Trail goes right to Floyd
      Hawver Road, and the yellow-blazed Colgate Lake Trail goes left to
      Colgate Lake. There is a good campsite here and a spring 0.3 mi. down
      the Dutcher Notch Trail. Continue ahead on blue trail. Climb steeply,
      passing over small crest called Arizona (3400 ft.).
10.0 South crest of Blackhead Mountain.
10.2 Summit of Blackhead (3937 ft.). (Yellow trail to the left goes to Black
      Dome and Thomas Cole Mountains.) The blue trail continues to the right
      and descends very steeply.
10.7 Yellow Jacket Lookout with its excellent views towards Albany and the
      Hudson Valley; continue steep descent.
11.2 Reach junction of the blue and yellow trails. (The yellow-blazed Batavia
      Kill Trail on the left leads steadily downhill 0.2 mi. to the Batavia
      Kill Lean-to and stream. It continues down to Big Hollow Road and the
      parking area at 1.5 mi.)

SECTION 23   Batavia Kill to Windham—Route 23

FEATURE: Windham High Peak   MAPS: LP Map #8
                                                        TC Map #41
DISTANCE: 9.5 miles   WB Map #13
                                                        HR Map #63
GENERAL DESCRIPTION:

Currently the last section of the Long Path, it continues on the blue-blazed
Escarpment Trail to its northern terminus at Windham, climbing over two peaks
and passing scenic outlooks.

FACILITIES:

    Parking   — Big Hollow Road, 1.5 mi. from the junction of the Long Path and
                 the Batavia Kill Trail (0.0 mi.)
              — Windham (9.5 mi.)

    Water   — Batavia Kill Lean-to (0.0 mi.)
              — Elm Ridge Lean-to (8.5 mi.)
              — Windham (9.5 mi.)

    Food   — Windham (9.5 mi.)
              — Maplecrest, 2.5 mi. on Elm Ridge Trail and Peck Road (8.5 mi.)

    Phone   — Windham (9.5 mi.)

    Lodging   — Windham (9.5 mi.)
              — Maplecrest, 2.5 mi. on Elm Ridge Trail and Peck Road (8.5 mi.)

    Camping   — Batavia Kill Lean-to, 0.2 mi. on the Batavia Kill Trail (0.0
                 mi.)
              — Elm Ridge Lean-to (8.5 mi.)

ACCESS:

New York State Thruway, exit 21, west on Route 23 to Windham, south on Route
296, then turn onto County Road 40 to the village of Maple Crest (general store
and hotels here). Turn left on Main Street (Route 56) which becomes Big Hollow
Road (the DEC "Catskill Trails" guide incorrectly calls this street Maple Crest
Road). Follow this road past the county recreation area to the end where there
is a parking area (a red-blazed trail comes in on the left just before the
parking area) and a spring just beyond on the right. To pick up the Long Path,
continue straight ahead (on foot) on the road to the trail junction and follow
the yellow-blazed Batavia Kill Trail 1.3 miles to the Batavia Kill Lean-to. At
1.5 miles, reach the junction with the blue-blazed Long Path. There is bus
service to Windham from New York City.

* * * * *

TRAIL DESCRIPTION:

0.0   From the junction with the yellow-blazed Batavia Kill Trail, continue
      ahead on BLUE-blazed Escarpment Trail.
3.0   Reach Acra Point (3085 ft.) and descend.
3.5   The red trail to the left leads (1.1 miles) to the end of Big Hollow Road
      and parking area. Continue on the blue-blazed trail.
6.5   Reach the summit of Windham High Peak (3524 ft.). Continue on past the
      lookout point.
8.5   The yellow-blazed trail to the right leads to a lookout. Just beyond is
      the Elm Ridge Lean-to. The yellow-blazed trail to the left just beyond
      the lean-to leads to a spring (0.1 mi.) and to Peck Road and Big Hollow
      Road (1.6 mi.). Follow the blue trail and descend.
9.5   Reach Route 23 and the current northern terminus of the Long Path.
      Opposite the trailhead across the highway is the parking area. Windham
      is 3 miles west.

o O o

MAP INDEX

Section	LP Map Number	TC Map Number	WB New York Walk Book Map Number	HR Hikers Region Map Number
1	1A	–	4	24
2	1B, 2	–	–	24, (2/8)*
3	2	–	–	(2/8)
4	2	–	–	(2/8)
5	2, 3	3	5	17
6	3	4	5, 6	17, 16
7	4	4	6, 8	4
8	4	8	8	18
9	4, 5	–	–	60
10	5	–	–	60
11	5	–	–	60
12	5	9	9, 10	41A, 65
13	5, 6	9	10, 11	41A, 61
14	6	43	11	61
15	6	43	11	61, 66
16	6	43	11, 12	66
17	6	42, 41	12, 13	66
18	7A	41	13	66, 25
19	7A	41	13	25, 71
20	7A	41	13	71, 35
21	7B	40, 41	13	35, 71
22	7B, 8	41	13	71, 63
23	8	41	13	63

*Maps 2/8 are now one map.

NOTES

NOTES

NOTES

Guide to the Long Path

NOTES

NEW YORK-NEW JERSEY TRAIL CONFERENCE

We are a non-profit federation of over 66 hiking clubs and over 5,000 individuals working together to build and maintain trails and promote conservation.

We have a long history
In 1920 the NY-NJ Trail Conference was formed when local hiking clubs gathered to plan a system of marking trails to make Bear Mountain-Harriman State Park more accessible to the public. In this same park, Trail Conference founders constructed and opened the first section of the Appalachian Trail in 1923. During the Thirties more trails were built and a system of trail maintenance was developed, giving each hiking club a share of responsibility. Today this maintenance network covers over 800 miles of marked trails from the Connecticut border to the Delaware Water Gap.

What we stand for
Volunteers of the Trail Conference work together to advance these common goals:
  • building and maintaining trails and trail shelters in the metropolitan area of New York and New Jersey
  • promoting public interest in hiking and conservation
  • aiding in the protection of wildlands and wildlife

How to join
Just fill out the form and mail it to us with your check. Why not treat yourself and a friend to a Trail Conference gift membership or publication?

NEW YORK-NEW JERSEY TRAIL CONFERENCE 1920

232 MADISON AVENUE • NEW YORK, NY 10016 212-696-6800

Please count me as a member of the NY-NJ Trail Conference in the category indicated:

☐ Individual —$10
☐ Student or Retired —$7.50
☐ Family —$15
☐ Sponsor * —$30
☐ Contributor * —$75
☐ Life * —$200
☐ Gift —$_____

*As a Sponsor, Contributor or Life member, I am entitled to select one free book:
  ☐ *Day Walker*
  or
  ☐ *A Guide To Ski Touring in NY-NJ*

Name _____

Address _____

_____
(zip)

Tax deductible to the extent permitted by law.
Checks payable to "Trails"

How is the Trail Conference supported?
Our work is supported through membership dues, publication sales, private contributions, and hundreds of hours donated annually by volunteers.

What your membership means
Your dues and contributions help carry on the work of the New York-New Jersey Trail Conference. **As a member you will receive the Trail Walker,** our bi-monthly newspaper full of information about new or relocated trails, reports of land acquisitions and threats to hiking areas, conservation news, tips for hikers, a listing of hikes open to Conference members and news of hiking club activities. **You'll be able to purchase our maps, books and guides at a discount,** and use our **telephone Alert service** for information on park closings, hiking conditions and emergencies. **You can participate with us** in creating new trails, maintaining the 800 miles of blazed trails, and taking part in Trail Conference activities.

I'm already a member of a hiking club. Isn't that enough? If you want a strong voice speaking for the interests of hiking and conservation, if you want a cooperative effort for building and maintaining trails to continue; if you want quality maps and guides… then your individual support of the Trail Conference is vital.

TRAIL CONFERENCE PUBLICATIONS

Maps
Waterproof, Tearproof Maps, In Four Colors
Latest Trails, Convenient Size, Fan Folded
Bear Mt.-Harriman State Park
Two Maps, 100 ft. contours, fully indexed.
East Hudson Trails
Three Maps—Canada Hill, Taurus to Beacon, Fahnestock Park. Contours of 100 ft. Historical notes.
North Jersey Trails
Two Maps. Wawayanda, Hewitt, Ringwood, Ramapo, Newark Watershed. etc. 65 trails.

Catskill Trails
Five Maps. Entire Catskill Park with complete trail index and guide on map backs. 100 ft. contours, state land boundaries.
Shawangunk Trails
Three maps. Mohonk and Minnewaska areas, blow up of Lake Mohonk area, 100 ft. contours, history.
Guides
Guide to Ski-Touring—29 Areas in New York and New Jersey. Where to go, how to get there, grade of difficulty, facilities, maps.
New York Walk Book
New Fifth edition of the indispensible reference book for the regional hiker. Index, maps included.
Guide to the Long Path
Sections conveniently broken down into day hikes, including maps.
Appalachian Trail Guide for New York-New Jersey
Latest edition of guide with maps.
Day Walker
Diverse range of 28 different day walks in New York metropolitan area.
Also Trail Conference T-Shirts, Patches and Decals.